Mu:

and Worship:

Principles to Practice

by
Peter Moger
Assistant Curate, Parish of Whitby

GROVE BOOKS LIMITED
Bramcote   Nottingham   NG9 3DS

CONTENTS

THE COVER PICTURE
is by Peter Ashton

ACKNOWLEDGEMENTS

I should like to thank all who have encouraged me in the preparation of this booklet: the Revs. Michael Vasey, Christopher Jones and Ben de la Mare for their help with my earlier dissertation *Music-Theology-Worship*; Canon Jane Sinclair and the Rev. Jeremy Fletcher for helpful editorial suggestions; and my wife Heather for her comments, proof-reading and loving support.

INTRODUCTION

It has long been acknowledged that a close relationship exists between music and theology. Yet most Christian discussion of music is concerned solely with music within the context of worship. There is a need, therefore, for a theological critique of music *per se*, and a subsequent application of theological principles to music for worship. This booklet aims to suggest such principles, and to consider how these might be put into practice within the worship of the Church.

First Impression January 1994

ISSN 0305-3067

ISBN 1 85174 257 3

1. MUSIC IN THE BIBLE AND CHRISTIAN TRADITION

The Bible

Although the Bible lacks direct reference to music's theological nature and purpose, music occupies a significant place within it. It is used to heighten key moments in God's dealings with creation, e.g. the birth of the created order (Job 38.7), the birth of the nation Israel (Exodus 15.1-18), the birth of Christ (Luke 2.14), and the birth of the new creation (Revelation 5.12f). Such music has a symbolic function. The trumpet, for instance, is used to herald God's encounter with Moses on Sinai (Exodus 19.13, 16, 19), and as a symbol of God's voice (Revelation 1.10; 4.1). It has a crucial role to play as Israel enters upon its inheritance at Jericho (Joshua 6.20), and will similarly call the New Israel to its inheritance at the coming of the Son of man (Matthew 24.31). It heralds judgement and calls to repentance, both at the Day of Atonement (Leviticus 25.9) and at the Day of Resurrection (1 Corinthians 15.52, 1 Thessalonians 4.16).

The Bible also records the musical expression of Jewish and Christian worship. An account of David's appointment of professional musicians for the Temple is given in 1 Chronicles 15. The greatest concentration of references to music for worship (both vocal and instrumental), though, occurs in the Psalter (e.g. Psalms 33.23; 40.3; 96.1; 98.1; 144.9; 150). The New Testament makes no mention of instrumental music in worship—something which contributed to subsequent suspicion of instruments by the Fathers and some reformers. That the worship of the early Church included music, however, is clear from passages such as Colossians 3.16b and Ephesians 5.19.

The New Testament includes several texts which have been identified as early Christian canticles and hymns. Among these are: in Luke, *Magnificat* (1.46-55), *Benedictus* (1.67-79), *Gloria in Excelsis* (2.14) and *Nunc Dimittis* (2.29-32); a number of Christological hymns in the epistles (e.g. Philippians 2.6-11, Colossians 1.15-20); and the songs of the redeemed in Revelation (4.8, 11; 5.9-10, 12; 14.3).

It is significant, though, that in the Bible music is not confined to the realm of the 'sacred'. In the Old Testament music is present as much in 'secular' life as in 'sacred'.[1] For the Jews, all life was life under the terms of the Covenant. Hence 'secular' music was no less 'religious' than that specifically associated with the cult. This Biblical view of music contrasts sharply with current assumptions about distinctions between 'sacred' and 'secular', and has a significant contribution to make in any debate about music and theology.

Patristic and Medieval Attitudes

Although Biblical evidence points to music's use in early Christian worship, the Fathers were ambivalent about it. Patristic condemnations of instrumental music abound, and are perhaps typified by Chrysostom's comments that 'where aulos players are, there Christ can never be'.[2] Chrysostom's objection was principally due to aulos-players' association

---

[1] Edgar (pp.48-49) has listed references to Jewish 'secular' music and has discovered work songs, music for war, marching and victory, songs for instruction, love songs, entertainment, music for dance, songs of derision, mourning and lamentation.

[2] Quoted by Van der Leeuw, p.227.

3

with magical arts and sexual immorality. Nevertheless, his writings also reveal an underlying dualism: he saw music as belonging to the 'lower' sensual (and pagan) nature, and thereby incompatible with the 'higher' nature of the Spirit. He is also guilty of issuing a blanket condemnation of all music, regardless of right or wrong use.

Chrysostom's attitude was reinforced by the rise of asceticism which, compounded with ecclesiastical legislation, led to the Church discriminating against instrumentalists.[1] Biblical references to musical instruments were dismissed either by allegorical interpretation, or by conceding that while the Jews were allowed instruments as an aid to piety, for Christians they were incompatible with 'spiritual worship'. It is hardly surprising, therefore, that early Christian music was exclusively vocal, though this must not been seen as such a discontinuity with Jewish tradition as is often thought.[2]

A more deep-seated objection to music in general concerned its power over human emotion. Augustine was no stranger to this. On hearing the antiphonal hymnody at Milan, he wrote:
'The tears flowed from me when I heard your hymns and canticles, for the sweet singing of your Church moved me deeply. The music surged in my ears, truth seeped into my heart, and my feelings of devotion overflowed, so that the tears streamed down.'[3]
Nevertheless he was cautious about music's emotional impact, and feared its misuse, lest it obscure rather than enhance the meaning of words. Augustine favoured singing in church as an aid to devotion, but was aware of the 'sin' of being moved more by the singing than by what was sung. In his treatise *De musica libri sex*, Augustine justifies the study of music as a means of divine contemplation—a conclusion based on Pythagoras' claim that the acoustic proportions of music are identical to the foundational proportions of the universe. For Augustine, earthly music was an image of heavenly music, and a vehicle of the soul's mystical return to God.

Medieval theologians continued to hold that music reflects the divine order. Medieval music theory, deriving largely from the *musica mathematica* of earlier theorists such as Boethius, saw in music a means of approaching the mystery of creation. God was believed to have created the world according to the laws of music, and human music was held to have a representative significance within creation, with composition being seen as mirroring God's act of creation.[4] The writings of Aquinas endorse this view. He reasoned that, as music reflected the divine order, it was logical that it should be the medium of worship, especially given its

[1] Aulos and kithara players are known to have been refused baptism.
[2] While the Temple used instruments in its worship, synagogue worship did not. The early Christians may be seen as continuing the practice of the synagogue rather than opposing that of the Temple. See Foley, p.29 *passim*.
[3] *Confessions*, IX, 6, 14.
[4] Despite the rise of humanism at the Renaissance, the influence of *musica mathematica* persisted. Michael Praetorius (*Syntagma Musicum*, 1614-19, III.59) pleaded that 'equality of measure . . . be preserved, . . . for to sing without rule and measure is to offend God himself, who arranged all things by number, weight and measure'.

known ability to direct human affections towards God. Nevertheless, for Aquinas, music was clearly a lesser science than doctrine, and medieval polemic against musical instruments was strong, with *verbatim* quotation of patristic writings.

The Reformation

Although individual protestant reformers' views on music varied, all were to some extent cautious about allowing it too free a rein in worship. Their concern was that, while music might point beyond itself to the reality of God, it can all too easily become an end in itself. The most radical view was that of Zwingli, ironically the most musically gifted of the reformers. He thought all music a distraction to worship, and considered congregational hymn singing unscriptural. Music was for Zwingli a 'secular' activity: hence it was permitted for private enjoyment but not for worship.

Calvin's stance was less rigid. He affirmed music's divine origin, but was wary of its possible malign influence on human behaviour. Hence he allowed music a limited ecclesiatical function, admitting that:

'singing has great strength and vigour to move and influence the hearts of men to invoke and praise God with a more vehement and ardent zeal'.[1]

His toleration of music, however, extended only to unaccompanied metrical psalms, the simplicity of which enabled texts to be heard and understood without confusion.[2]

Calvin's approach to music was 'functional' in that it was largely concerned with music's use. Luther, in contrast, adopted an 'ontological' approach. As a discipline, he placed it 'next to theology', and promoted its use in worship. Luther was unequivocal about music's divine origin, seeing it as a divine gift which comes to humankind through hearing. This suggested a parallel between music and the gospel: both have a heavenly origin and come to us through the voice. Music and theology, claimed Luther, inform one another.

His principal emphasis, though, was on music's 'declarative' character: its ability to 'make known'. This had an outworking both in a functional sense within Lutheran worship, where it was used as a powerful vehicle for the proclamation of the gospel[3], and in an ontological sense, in that music may be held to 'make known' aspects of the creation which cannot be communicated through the word alone.[4] Hence Luther avoided Calvin's trap of regarding music purely as the servant of a text. While acknowledging that it may bring an added dimension to the word, Luther affirmed music for its own sake as praise of God and worship *per se*.

Enlightenment and Modernity

Since the Reformation, the relationship between music and theology has been less readily acknowledged, with most discussion focussing on the

---

[1] Quoted by Leaver, *Marbeck*, p.55f.
[2] Calvin is largely responsible for the influential and enduring view that (church) music exists as the servant of a text, and not as music *per se*.
[3] See Leaver, *MP*.
[4] Luther defended instrumental music against Calvinists on the grounds that music communicates meaning without the need for a text.

specific issue of music in worship. This has been largely due both to an increasing compartmentalization of thought, and to a narrowing of outlook on the place of the arts in society. Music is today treated superficially: as a diversion, a background, a means of recreation.[1] Since the Enlightenment has come a marginalization of music's place in Western thought and society, and a widening gulf between 'sacred' and 'secular'.

The classical-medieval heritage of *musica mathematica* has resurfaced at various times[3] as a valuable reminder of music's relationship to the transcendent. But perhaps the most significant contribution to the debate in the nineteenth century came from Schopenhauer. He maintained that all music is religious in the sense that it offers direct aural expression of ultimate reality.[3]

This has opened up the vital question of whether one can speak of 'religious music'. Some theologians, taking their lead from Schopenhauer, are willing to acknowledge a religious dimension in all music[4], and some even go as far as to venture that 'all good art . . . is implicitly Christian'.[5] Others are more cautious, and reserve the use of the term 'religious' for music composed specifically for sacred use. Such a view, though, considers music solely in functional terms and fails to take account of the clear ontological emphasis of much Biblical and traditional Christian material. Another possible use of the term is for music which is self-consciously 'religious' or 'Christian'.[6] Against this one must set the possibility that music which is not consciously 'religious' might still praise God. This is the opinion of Barth, who writes of Mozart that he:

> 'does not intend to proclaim the praise of God. He just does so in fact; precisely in the humility in which he . . . lets be heard what he apparently hears, that which impresses itself on him from God's creation which rises up in him and demands to proceed out of him'.[7]

It is a common, but misguided, assumption among Christians that they alone can produce truly 'good' art. It is a mistake to assume that religious belief is a necessary qualification for the production of great religious art, or that the Holy Spirit is active in inspiration only within the walls of the Church.[8]

If music's theological implications are to be taken seriously, efforts must be made to express a cohesive working theology of music, which can be used as a basis for evaluation and criticism, and as a foundation for discussion of music's place in Christian worship.

---

[1] The development of concert halls during the last 200 years bears witness to this.
[2] e.g. J. S. Bach's use of numerological devices to give symbolic expression to the theological convictions which undergird his music; and, more recently Paul Hindemith, who recovered certain Pythagorean insights.
[3] Schopenhauer claimed that if 'we could put what music expresses into concepts, this would be the final revelation in words of reality as it is in itself, independent of all representation' (Bryan Magee, 'Schopenhauer, Arthur' in *NG*, vol.16, p.733).
[4] e.g. Van der Leeuw (pp.259-262) who writes that 'the point where religion and music touch can be found in every sort of music'.
[5] Griffiths, pp.5-9. This also raises the question as to whether 'religious' music is necessarily 'good' music, or music 'used aright'.
[6] J. S. Bach's music, for instance, would fall within this category.
[7] Barth, p.27.
[8] *WBHS*, p.163f.

2. TOWARDS A THEOLOGY OF MUSIC

Music's Origins and Status
Music is a universal phenomenon, and many see it as part of the natural order: bird song being as much music as that of human invention. One might propose, therefore, that music has its *origin in God*, though exactly how it might be said to 'originate in God' is debatable. Some argue that Biblical evidence denies music's direct divine origin, and suggest that it is an essentially creaturely activity.[1] Holders of this opinion dismiss the view that music is found in nature as a misguided post-Enlightenment assumption. But this stance is questionable, not least in that it fails to consider the important legacy of *musica mathematica* which retains validity in principle (if not in detail) in modern discussions of music and theology.[2] One must also concede that if creatures are the originators of music, they are nevertheless God's creatures (and, if human, created in his image)— something which in some sense implies an ultimate divine authorship of the arts.

A common modern assumption is that music is a luxury, and that the arts are surplus to basic human needs: an assumption bolstered by the functional orientation of modern Western society. Yet music's universality, its significance in people's lives, its psychological power, and its ability to influence human behaviour, call this assumption into question, and suggest that music is at very least, important. A Christian view of music maintains that it is a *creative necessity*. The instinct for creativity, which all human beings possess, is part of the *imago Dei*. To relegate the arts to the status of non-necessity is to deny them their rightful place in the divine order. They emanate originally from God, who is a God of overflow and blessing, beyond the level of basic need.[3] God wills human beings to function not at a basic level but at a truly human level, and to be truly human is to be true to the creator's image.

Music, God and Creation
Christian theology holds that the universe exhibits an order which bears witness to the God who created it. If music is to honour God, and be part of his ongoing work of creation through human agency, it should *reflect the order of creation*. Much contemporary music is written with the express intention of denying order. The principle of indeterminacy[4] is, by definition, dedicated to disorder. It assumes that music—a human activity—is a random event in an accidental universe. By sharp contrast, jazz involves a fusion of randomness (through improvization) and determinism (through convention), and offers what is perhaps a more accurate reflection of the universe as it is. Hardy and Ford have identified randomness in jazz as a manifestation of 'non-order' (i.e. neither rigidly determined, nor opposed to order). This understanding of 'non-order', and 'order' might be a helpful foil to an 'order/disorder' dualism.

[1] Edgar (p.29) claims that 'nature does not generate music independently of human beings', using Genesis 4.21 to support his view.
[2] It points to God as both source and goal of music, and thereby opposes modernity's claim that music is an *ex nihilo* creation of the human spirit.
[3] Hardy and Ford, p.81.
[4] That in which organisation is left to chance (e.g. by tossing of coins).

Christian theology also asserts that the universe is *contingent*: that it points away from itself, to its creator (Psalms 19.1; 96.11-12). Music, as part of the created order, points to God and reveals something of him.[1] This has important implications. If music's purpose is to point to God, this precludes Romantic notions of music as an end in itself.

If music is held to express divine attributes, one is faced with a problem of subjectivity. (Indeed, one could argue that all evaluations of music are ultimately subjective and/or culturally relative.) It is important that this inevitable subjectivity is balanced by the objective picture of God and the world which Christian theology presents. This gives us 'every reason to believe that music is quite capable of giving voice to . . . fundamental truths'[2], and that 'the experience of beauty . . . in music, is deeply related to ultimate reality, to God's presence and his plan for us'.[3]

Christianity also claims that God creates out of love, and that he affirms his creation—most supremely in the Incarnation. Music, as part of this 'physical' world, is *affirmed*. This allows no room for the dualism that rejects music as 'worldly' and distinct from the 'higher' things of the Spirit.

The role of human beings within creation is that of stewards, with a mandate to *develop* what is given (Genesis 1.28). Hence a composer has a responsibility to respect the 'raw materials' of sound (e.g. the harmonic series, etc.). The development of these 'givens' has implications not only for musicians but also for listeners in coming to terms with what is new. As a creative steward the musician has a duty to work for God's glory and for the building up of fellow human beings. The Romantic image of an artist bent on self-fulfilment is clearly at odds with this.

Finally, Christianity holds the hope of the *redemption* of the created order, through which good will overcome evil, and order disorder. Begbie has suggested that music which is true to the Christian pattern of creation-fall-redemption will display both honesty and hope: honesty at the reality of evil, yet hope that disorder will give way to order.[4] Much music communicates a sense of unmitigated despair: it is honest, yet lacks hope. Conversely, some music attempts to convey hope, without being honest about the world as it is. This criticism may be levelled at much modern 'Christian music', some of which demonstrates appalling superficiality.

Music's Meaning and Purpose
A common modern assumption is that art has no meaning outside itself: a 'formalist' view enshrined in the music of Boulez and others who have followed the 'total serial' path since 1945. While such a position might appear strictly untenable—for it fails to take account of the effect of human organisation on music—the opposite view (that music exists merely as a medium for a message) appears equally false. One cannot separate music's 'meaning' from the music itself. It is often assumed that

[1] One must avoid the temptation to suggest that music can offer an objective reflection of aspects of God's nature (see *ITWH* 59).
[2] Begbie, *Music*, p.5.
[3] Edgar, p.133.
[4] Begbie, *Music*, p.17f.

music is sonically neutral. However, the meaning of a piece of music *is* conveyed in its sonic structure.[1] This has important implications for the use of music in Christian worship. It is vital that music is evaluated in its own right, avoiding the temptation to see it either as purely message-orientated, or entirely meaningless outside its own internal organization. It is also important to remember that a piece of music will not 'mean' the same in two different cultures. Music is a 'language', yet it is not a universal language. Cultural conditioning counts for a great deal.

A major theological premise is that, as part of a contingent created order, music's primary purpose is to glorify God. Those without religious belief typically hold that it exists for the purpose of enjoyment. For the theologian, these two views are compatible and complementary. For if music points to God, the source of goodness, blessing and delight, it is natural that it should be enjoyed by human beings. The question remains whether music not written expressly for God's glorification does in fact do so; and whether human enjoyment of music is not at times in danger of becoming veneration.

Music is often recognized as a means of communication, both in itself and as the bearer of words. Music can enhance a text and help draw out its meaning. Over-emphasis of music as the servant of a text, though, can lead to the destruction of artistic form[2] (cf. Calvin and Luther). Another major purpose lies in its ability to influence feeling, although the specific nature of the relationship between music and emotion is unclear. Music is one of the profoundest influences on emotion (virtually all people respond to it) and a significant proportion of Biblical references to music link it with feeling.[3] Music's emotional impact depends on a whole network of factors, not least its relation to human experience in the world.

Misuse and Redemption
Despite possible uses for good, since music is exercised by fallen human beings, its misuse and corruption are real possibilities. At a basic level, it is open to trivialization, as background 'muzak', for instance. At a more complex level, it may be abused to the extent that it gives expression to that which is evil.

The use of music to 'express' good or evil is difficult to define, as music so often reflects the attitudes and states of mind of those who create it. An especially pervasive force in music is the 'association of ideas' it generates in performers and listeners (e.g. Wagner's music, with its strong pagan connotations; some rock music, with its links with the occult and drug culture; and New Age music which can function as an anaesthetic). Certain associations of ideas may cause music to be negative and harmful rather than positive and beneficial.

[1] See Cooke. Begbie (*Music*, p.6) illustrates this well: 'An aesthetically inept song remains inept however scriptural the words might be'.
[2] Griffiths (p.5) writes that Christian art so often fails 'because its creators are too full of the desire to get across a clear and conscious message'.
[3] e.g. 1 Samuel 16.23, 2 Kings 3.15, Psalms 45.8; 71.22; 92.1-4. N.B. the impossibility of 'singing the Lord's song in a strange land' (Psalm 137.4), where the correct response to the pain of the exile is an absence of music.

But does music have intrinsic power to manipulate a person's state of mind? An examination of David's calming of Saul (1 Samuel 16.14-23), shows that while the music was important in securing the desired purpose, it was effective only when coupled with faith on the part of Saul. This might suggest that music's power may be either affirmed or resisted by faith and that, while it is a powerful means of achieving a purpose, it is not intrinsically manipulative.

In what sense, then, can music be 'evil'? If one accepts that a piece of music may be reduced to its constituent parts, it would appear that the 'evil' cannot be contained within individual notes or rhythms. It might be in the music's structure, or compositional features—but even these are usually reducible to their components. Perhaps a more satisfactory answer might be that the 'evil' is part of the composer's outlook. One of the effects of modernity has been a move towards a more individualistic, and salvific, view of art. With the rise and subsequent influence of Romanticism, extravagant claims have been made for music as a means of direct access to God.

In the present century art has largely replaced the Christian belief in God, and aesthetic language has become a substitute for theological langauge. The Biblical view of art is of a creative activity undertaken in response to God, but always secondary to humanity's primary purpose of worshipping God. When this primary purpose is lost, art can become a God-substitute, and be idolized as the locus of salvation. The presence of 'negative spiritual forces' or 'evil' in music might be attributable to this root cause: that of idolatry and the abandonment of the Godward dimension of the creative dynamic.

A Christian theology of music must take seriously the future hope of redemption.[1] A view of music as a gift of God in creation (as opposed to a human enterprise) allows, despite misuse, for future redemption along with the rest of the universe. Romans 8.18-23, which speaks of the whole creation 'groaning in travail' and awaiting the future hope, can be applied to music as to any other part of the created order. Meanwhile, human beings are charged with the responsible stewardship of music, and its use for good where possible.

---

[1] N.B. The dangers of an over-realized eschatology in music (see ch.4).

3. MUSIC AND WORSHIP

Christian Worship and Music

Within human nature is the instinct to worship. Central to Christianity is a recognition that God is worthy of worship, and that he 'desires and enables us to offer it'.[1] Worship is normative and generative for the Christian community, enabling the formation of bonds among human beings and with God. Whatever other purposes worship might serve, these are secondary to its main purpose of glorifying God.

Knowing God is 'inseparable from praising him'.[2] Hence music has an important role in making God known through worship. There is a reciprocity in worship: we offer to God, and God gives back to us.[3] If music is regarded as a necessity, it will be seen as an integral part of worship, not a dispensable adjunct. Worship without music, while not invalid, appears to be lacking in some way. The Biblical account of the origins of worship and culture (Genesis 4), shows the importance of both. To assert worship as 'spiritual' and culture as 'material' is to fall prey to dualism.

The act of 'singing to the Lord' forms part of a basic human religious instinct. Singing can transform words into a new level of expression, but without detracting from their essential meaning. Hence it has a vital place in worship, revealing it 'to be an affair of the whole person, mind, heart, voice, body'.[4]

In the Bible one may discern two strands of sacred music. There is the 'spontaneous' music of Saul and David, and the 'ordered' liturgical music of Levi and Asaph. The first points to the common life of the community of faith, the second to the 'otherness' of worship. There is a need for a healthy tension between the two.[5]

The 'spontaneous' strand has seen a recent resurgence in historic denominations through charismatic renewal. One hallmark of this spontaneity is the phenomenon of 'singing in the Spirit'. It is significant in that it is neither 'controlled' nor 'out of control'. As such it may be seen as a manifestation of 'non-order'[6], and a valuable foil to 'ordered' liturgical worship.

The reciprocal relationship between music and theology must be recognized within the context of worship. If music becomes detached from its theological roots, it can easily become entertainment. Likewise,

---

[1] *ITWH*, 71.
[2] Hardy and Ford, p.25.
[3] '[God] accepts the offering of our hymns, songs, anthems and settings and returns it to us transformed and enriched for our benefit. This may be so as to reveal something of himself, and in order that we may have a glimpse of heaven' (*ITWH*, 89).
[4] Wainwright, p.200.
[5] Spontaneity is not necessarily to be equated with 'of the Spirit' (Buchanan, p.11f).
[6] See ch.2. For the trained musician, singing in the Spirit is an enigma. One might expect a group of largely non-musical people singing 'spontaneously' to produce something chaotic and dissonant. The result, however, is harmonious and, at times, technically intricate. It is fascinating that people who cannot normally sing in tune can do so when singing in the Spirit.

The reciprocal relationship between music and theology must be recognized within the context of worship. If music becomes detached from its theological roots, it can easily become entertainment. Likewise, theology without music can become arid and soulless. Church music is functional, but is also connected to the theological framework of Christian worship, life and witness. In practice, though, there is a considerable gulf between theology and church music. Criticism of church music often lacks theological substance—a symptom of what has been called 'a fundamental deficiency in the spirituality from which Western Christians compose and use music in worship'[1] This spirituality has produced worship which is triumphalist, escapist and insufficiently 'earthed', with such deficiences being present in the music.

If music's primary purpose is to glorify God, its role in worship is no different, especially as it is here offered as a conscious expression of praise. The chief object of church music is not musical: there is no room in worship for music as an end in itself. An exaggeration of music's importance can undermine worship's Christocentricity: church music is the servant of the Christ at the centre of worship.

A view of church music as praise of God holds to an ontological understanding of music—that it exists regardless of any extraneous function. Nevertheless, it has an important communicative role: usually through the illumination of words. To hold the primacy of this role, though, is to undermine music's ontological status. Church music also communicates prophetically—as a vehicle of forthtelling. Hence the parallel between music and preaching. This realization was central to Luther's theology of music, and enables justice to be done to music's declarative potential independent of any text.

As a vehicle for the expression of feeling, church music has a major role to play. A renewed concern for the expression of feeling in worship has been a welcome feature of renewal. Such an emphasis, though, can easily degenerate into a concern for self-expression. Feeling must be balanced by the objective 'givens' of Scripture and tradition. Music can help provide this balance.

Participation
Worship is the concern of the whole Church. An understanding of the priesthood of all Christians holds that worship should serve the needs of the whole body. Hence music performed by an organist, choir or music group has the task of enabling the worship of all present. Musicians, while different in function from other worshippers, are no different in status.

'Participation' has been a keyword in recent Roman Catholic discussion of the liturgy. Pope Pius X's use of the phrase 'active participation' (1903) led to considerable debate of congregational liturgical and musical involvement, with participation becoming a major theme in the discussions of the Second Vatican Council.[2] It is a misconception, though,

[1] Cray in Sheldon, p.12.
[2] See McManus.

that active participation is a necessary ingredient of active worship. The English cathedral tradition, in which the choir sings on behalf of all present, enables worship through reflective participation, the value and importance of which should not be denied.[1]

Opinion on congregational musical participation is divided. Some claim that only music in which all can join is suitable for worship. Others stress that over-participation denies the use of reflective faculties. Advocates of maximum active participation[2] have claimed that the Church has encouraged the passive culture of the present age by promoting 'non-participatory worship'. Such a view is difficult to sustain, since 'non-participatory worship' is presumably a contradiction in terms. There should be room for both active and reflective participation. The success of Taizé music, which offers worshippers a balance of action and reflection, suggests that this message is taking root.

In Genesis 4, the music referred to is instrumental, not vocal.[3] This might suggest that while all may sing (i.e. music is for everyone), only some (those with specialist ability) are called to be 'musicians'. The specific practice of music is therefore a divine vocation. It is insufficient, though, to view the practice of church music in purely functional terms. A church musician is a liturgical theologian, a person whose ministry grows out of faith and is exercised in the power of the Holy Spirit. Church musicians, should be qualified musically and spiritually. There has long been a mistrust of 'professionalism' in church music, and while church musicians are not 'romantic' artists bent on self-expression, this is no licence for mediocrity. The Church's worship will only ever be a poor echo of the worship of heaven—and musicians should strive continually for greater competence.

Hymns and Songs: Music as a vehicle of theological influence
Within church music, hymns and songs have a special place. Their accessibility, participatory nature and memorability, facilitate a profound influence upon faith and life. The phrase *lex orandi—lex credendi* may aptly be applied to hymnody. Leslie Olive writes:
  '. . . what we sing is important to us, and, when we sing something often, it becomes part of us and part of the way we view things'.[4]
The potency of words and music combined makes hymns and songs lodge more easily in the consciousness than other forms of words. When used in worship, the combination of words and music can help shape our perceptions of God.

Participation in singing is therefore a powerful means of theological teaching.[5] John Wesley realized this and wrote of his 1780 hymn book as being 'a body of experimental and practical divinity'. One can overplay the

---

[1] Christopher Dearnley in Sheldon, p.119.
[2] e.g. Philip Lawson-Johnston in Sheldon, p.161.
[3] Edgar, p.100f.
[4] Olive, p.6.
[5] Leach (p.40) claims that people learn doctrine more through what they sing than through what they hear, and Begbie (*Spirituality*, pp.227-239) draws attention to the 'significant role' sung music can play 'in educating congregations and shaping theological awareness'.

educative role of sung worship—many people probably remember the tune (and general drift) of a hymn or song more than its actual words. Nevertheless, the enduring popularity of hymns and songs both inside and outside the Church suggests that they be taken seriously, as a means of theological influence, and a vehicle of mission.

Wainwright writes that 'the Christian hymn may perhaps be considered as a sung confession of faith'.[1] The hymns of Wesley and Watts certainly provide valuable windows onto Methodist and Puritan doctrine. Some hymnwriters (and a substantial proportion of modern songwriters) have integrated Scripture into their texts, with the intention of helping Biblical verses lodge in the mind. Alongside the doctrinal and scriptural content of hymnody lies an important existential element—through which the Christian is enabled to further his/her growth in grace (e.g. the final verse of Watts' *When I survey the wondrous Cross*).

Music 'readily unites among themselves the members of a single social community'.[2] Hence the music of any worshipping group can easily contribute to an implicit theology, which runs parallel to the explicit theology of readings, sermons and liturgy, and may either support it, or run counter to it. An announcment, well into a service, that 'we shall now have a time of worship' raises important questions about what has been taking place beforehand, during the service and before it as well. The implicit message here is that 'worship' consists in the singing of a particular type of song.

Worship songs are markedly different from hymns and require different criteria of assessment. There are many varieties of song—Begbie[3] has isolated six distinct types—but central to them all is a conviction that worship has to do with a personal relationship between the worshipper and God. One might differentiate between hymns sung *about* God and songs addressed *to* God. This is sometimes a false distinction, but it does highlight a major difference between the two.

Many worship songs lack substantial theological content. Arguably they make greater sense when placed within a worship context, but sometimes the words themselves could realistically be sung by anyone, regardless of their faith. Some texts make no mention of God, while a large number are guilty of sentimentalism. To examine only the words of a worship song, though, is to miss the point. They need to be put with their music, and then sung by a congregation which longs to express itself through singing. The cerebral content assumes less of a priority in songs than in hymns. Nevertheless, it is a mistake to assume that any hymn or song may be reduced to its words: it is a composite musico-linguistic entity. Nor must one ignore music's theological impact. Begbie has written: 'the melodic, harmonic and rhythmic dimensions of music are all value-laden. Music imprints its own meaning, however hard this is to articulate'.[4] Compared with traditional hymns, worship songs become very easily embedded in the consciousness because they are short and sung repeatedly. Hence the power of a short song is considerable, and often greater than that of a reading or a sermon.

[1] Wainwright, p.183.
[2] Wainwright, p.215.
[3] Begbie *Spirituality*, p.231f.
[4] Ibid., p.230.

4. DISCERNING AN 'APPROPRIATE' MUSIC FOR WORSHIP

Deep divisions exist over what is considered 'appropriate' music for worship, and criteria of evaluation are hard to find. Vatican II (1964) merely pronounced that 'sacred music increases to holiness to the degree that it is intimately linked with liturgical action'. *In Tune with Heaven* offers helpful guidelines[1], but there is still work to be done in this area.

'Sacred' and 'Secular'

It is often assumed that there is a clear distinction between 'sacred' and 'secular' music. The Bible makes no such distinction, though this does not deny the appropriateness of certain types of music for specific occasions. The Biblical picture points to the religious significance of all life. Music should derive its character not from whether an aspect of life is deemed 'sacred' or 'secular' but from the circumstances in which it is used.

If music is part of a 'good' creation (and thereby able to foster the relationship between God and humanity), it makes little sense to distinguish between 'sacred' and 'secular'. Nevertheless, since the Enlightenment such distinction is generally taken for granted. Hence the suggestion that 'a secular musical idiom' might not be incompatible with 'a Christian view of life', and that in offering in worship music that is otherwise 'secular', such music may be consecrated or sanctified.[2]

The view that 'secular' music needs to be 'sanctified' for Christian use is widespread. One of its advocates, William Booth, the founder of the Salvation Army, asked: 'Why should the Devil have all the best tunes?' In so doing he followed others before him, notably Luther, who had aimed to provide accessible music for worship by 'borrowing' from popular culture. Booth's question reveals the underlying assumption that one can speak of 'the Devil's tunes'. It is important to guard against notions that the Devil has creative power, and to emphasize that his ability is limited to causing a misuse of God-given creativity.

Whereas in the past, stylistic differences between sacred and secular were minimal—witness Bach and Handel's frequent 'borrowings' between works—today the styles are clearly distinct, making transfers extremely complicated. The widening of the divide is usually traced back to the Enlightenment, though its roots may be seen in the sixteenth century, in a combination of the rise of humanism and the efforts of the more radical reformers.

A major resurgence of the 'sacred/secular' debate was fuelled by church music developments in the 1960s. The 'Twentieth Century Church Light Music Group' sought to provide new tunes in a popular 'secular' idiom for exisiting texts.[3] At around the same time, the compilers of *Youth Praise I*

[1] *ITWH*, pp.67-73.
[2] *Ibid.,* §69.
[3] The group aimed to do the same as Luther and Booth had done—to bridge the gap between church music and the musical tastes of the majority.

and II and (later) *Psalm Praise* set new and traditional words to 'secular' tunes. One notable instance is the suggestion that a version of Psalm 46[1] be sung to Eric Coates' *Dam Busters March*.[2]

One must ask whether music (e.g. the *Dam Busters March*) retains 'secular' associations when wedded to sacred words. Many people are uneasy about using obviously militaristic music for a Christian hymn.[3] Others claim that a 'secular' idiom (or tune), might be particularly apt in lending expression to a sacred text, as in the use of jazz-inspired idioms by Christopher Norton and others in more recent material.[4]

It is dangerous to assume that 'secular' music automatically sheds its connotations when transferred to a new context. Music is not sonically neutral and does not exist only as an available medium for a message. If we allow that a piece contains meaning within its sonic structure, this would preclude the 'sacred' use of certain music, and the composition of church music in certain styles. Against this, one might allow for the 'baptism' of music transferred from a secular to a sacred context—not in terms of a God/Devil dualism, but as an incarnational statement affirming music's inherent goodness, and claiming it for use in God's praise.

Style
The question of style in church music and the relative merits of different styles is complex. Not only are there many styles, but they are largely cultivated and enjoyed by distinct social groups. Discussion of style is often seen in terms of a polarization into 'low' and 'high' culture, with the (unspoken) assumption that 'low' culture lacks aesthetic validity. Against this, Edgar writes:
> '... popular culture can be as genuine and authentic as the high culture promoted by élitists ... [since it] is in touch with its audience in a way that high culture is not. High culture tends to be in touch with the creators instead.'[5]

As cultural differences are important, so is temperament. Preference for a particular style of music usually has more to do with temperament than with theological conviction. A mixed diet of musical styles in worship might not satisfy anyone completely but does at least give each worshipper at least one style with which to identify.

Cray sees a false assumption underlying much contemporary Christian music, namely that, by withdrawing from the world, it is thought possible to create specifically 'Christian' music. Against this he rightly asserts that there is 'no such thing as a musical form which is distinctively Christian'.[6] It is virtually impossible to separate style from content. Hence it is hard to

[1] *God is our Strength and Refuge* (Psalm Praise 91, Hymns for Today's Church 527).
[2] See also the setting of *What a friend we have in Jesus* to the tune *Now the carnival is over* (Youth Praise 2/240).
[3] Cf. the use of Elgar's 'Land of Hope and Glory' melody for the hymn *Glory in the Highest*. For some, the Elgar tune has distasteful imperialist associations which preclude its use in worship.
[4] *Songs from the Psalms* (Hodder & Stoughton, London, 1990) 13C, 130D.
[5] Edgar, p.113.
[6] Cray in Sheldon, p.22.

write rock music which does not carry certain connotations. To claim that style is neutral, and that it needs only to be filled with 'Christian content' is dangerous.

Discussion of style has assumed greater prominence in recent years with the more widespread use of popular idioms in worship. Some styles have been condemned by the establishment as banal, ephemeral and inappropriate. Nevertheless, the influence of 'popular' music in Christian worship has become increasingly pervasive. Today, few churches can claim to have been totally unaffected by it, even if they have not enthusiastically embraced it. Landmarks along the path of gradually increasing acceptance have been the moves towards contemporary liturgical language and greater informality in worship-leading. The idiom of most modern 'popular' church music is 'Radio 2 "easy listening" . . . with occasional forays into Radio 1'[1], yet instances exist (e.g. the '9 o'clock service' in Sheffield) where the rock idiom is axiomatic to the worship as a whole.

An 'appropriate' church music will, presumably, be an authentic vehicle of Christian communication. The Church is an historic movement and, if it is to communicate through music, that music must have some continuity with the art of the past. This is a pressing issue for post-Vatican II Roman Catholics who have had to discover a style for vernacular music almost overnight. Stephen Dean has observed that 'an exclusive reliance on music written in the last ten or twenty years is dangerous'[2]—a warning which applies equally to many charismatic churches which have abandoned traditional church music. As well as acknowledging the music of the past, for church music to communicate it must also take into account the prevailing culture, and address the need for 'indigenous authenticity'. This is never an easy task, given the wide range of taste and background, but necessary nevertheless.

These considerations apart, discussions about style are often inconclusive. Dean writes:
'If the underlying spiritual values of the community are sound, they will be able to find music that accords with them. No music which can be shown to serve as a prayer can be dismissed. Time will generally sort out the good from the bad'.[3]

Judgement: The 'Good' and The 'Bad'
The past 200 years have seen Western church music decline in status. Once influential, the Church is now 'the refuge for all the music unfit for theatre or concert hall'.[4] People accept in church music which they would never tolerate in a concert. It is often wrongly assumed that church music does not have to meet 'secular' standards. Church music stands under a double discipline: that of general musical quality, and that of the standard imposed by its special function of praising the creator.

[1] Begbie, *Spirituality*, p.233.
[2] Dean in Sheldon, p.43.
[3] *Ibid.,* p.47.
[4] Lang, p.1007.

One criterion used to determine music's suitability is its appeal to worshippers. This criterion is inevitably subjective. Much of the music of the late nineteenth century, and of the current renewal movement, is popular because of its instant appeal to the senses, while sadly lacking in theological and musical quality. Another criterion is accessibility. John Leach has written that a good standard of music for worship is essential, but understands 'good' as meaning 'accessible'.[1]. Accessibility is a positive feature of many worship songs which take seriously the need to connect with popular culture, and that 'in worship God engages with us as we are'.[2] One must beware of overplaying accessibility as a virtue, lest one lose the creative impetus towards taking new departures in church music and the broadening of worshippers' musical horizons.

Of overriding importance in the evaluation of any church music is its theological integrity. If music in general should display both honesty about the world and hope in God's redemptive purposes, so should church music. Few hymns, though, and fewer songs, are true to a full, realistic range of human emotions (and therefore compare unfavourably with the Psalms, in which life is presented with a brutal honesty.)[3] Much renewal music 'transmits a message of joy without tears, glory without suffering, resurrection without crucifixion'.[4] Human weakness is seldom acknowledged, sin and suffering are often dismissed. Church music must avoid the temptation to stay with the cosy and familiar, and if it is to be prophetic, it must disturb as well as console. Some more recent songs[5] might indicate a turning of the tide, with a greater willingness to address 'difficult' themes such as social injustice and spiritual emptiness.

The Christian hope receives ample coverage in hymns and songs— though many songs exude a feeling of a joy which runs only skin deep. The note of victory is sounded with great frequency, and is closely allied to a desire to sing of God's power—often in the context of spiritual warfare. Such songs can appear triumphalist and fail to acknowledge the Biblical theme of God's power demonstrated in weakness (1 Corinthians 2.2-5).

Robin Leaver has written of the importance of eschatology for church music, which 'has its roots in the past, its blossom in the present, and its fruits in the future'.[6] A major problem confronting church music today is the legacy of romanticism—a movement which has encouraged a view of art as an end in itself. The Christian alternative to romanticism is an eschatology with a clear future dimension. Romanticism has produced music which is self-referencing, and which offers instant gratification to

[1] Leach, p.82.
[2] Begbie, *Spirituality*, p.233.
[3] Hardy and Ford (p.37) write that the Psalms offer 'a vehicle for realistic but $jubilant joy in God, taking up the good and the bad into a faith that always (even if it takes a struggle) results in praise of God.
[4] Begbie, *Music*, p.18. Many popular nineteenth century evangelical hymns fall into the same trap.
[5] e.g. G. Kendrick, *O Lord, the clouds are gathering*, B. Woolett, *How long, O Lord?*.
[6] Leaver, in *Duty and Delight*, p.60.

the listener/worshipper, reflecting an over-realized eschatology. The marginalisation of a future eschatology within charismatic thinking, and the consequent shift of emphasis to the present activity of the Holy Spirit, has meant that, in some cases, renewal music has gone in this direction.

Good church music, regardless of style, will also display musical integrity. A pervasive attitude in today's Church is anti-aestheticism. Many see musical mediocrity as an indicator of a church's 'soundness', while high musical standards are often taken to indicate 'lifeless' worship. Richard Griffiths has observed that

'pop music, ... one of the most living of our art forms, seems to become afflicted with a maudlin mediocrity once it begins to be used for Christian purposes.'[1]

Musicians should strive for excellence as they seek to worship 'in Spirit and in truth' (John 4.24).

Renewal music is often dismissed as simplistic and second-rate. While simplicity is no bad thing, there should be no room in worship for the sub-standard. The majority of songs have predictable melodies, which fit into equally predictable phrase patterns (usually 4 or 8 bars), and employ a handful of chords. Such ingredients yield music which is easy on the ear yet makes little demand on the listener. This matter is as much theological as musical, and may be seen as a musical outworking of an over-realised eschatology. The predictability of such music offers instant gratification, and denies the all-important 'not yet' dimension of Christian life and faith.[2] There are, of course, exceptions.[3]

An encouraging sign in recent church music is the combination of the ideals of quality, simplicity and accessibility found in Taizé music. This music's flexibility is its great strength: it may be straightforward or complex according to the circumstances of performance and the forces available. It is easily sung by a congregation of average ability, yet offers opportunities for more demanding involvement by trained musicians. It is also virtually unique in its appeal across boundaries of nationality, culture, class and denomination.

Although a universally appropriate church music is impossible to define, one must try to evaluate what is suitable for use in Christian worship. These attempts will necessarily take into account cultural, temperamental and situational considerations. Questions of style—and perceived notions of 'sacred' and 'secular' are ultimately less important than the issue of judgement between good and bad. Good church music will display theological integrity and musical quality. Important, too, is the integrity of the act of worship as a whole, for church music is only one amongst many vehicles for the worship God's people.

[1] Griffiths, p.5.
[2] Begbie, *Spirituality*, p.238.
[3] Christopher Norton's songs never fail to interest and two of Kendrick's (*Meekness and Majesty* and *From Heaven You Came*) make use of interesting phrase lengths.

5. SELECTING AND USING MUSIC FOR WORSHIP

Criteria for Selection

Church music is both a theological indicator and a potential theological generator: all music has a theological emphasis. If church music is to glorify to God, one must adopt a scientific precision in questioning the theological integrity of the music we use.

The theological content of hymns and songs must be screened carefully, avoiding quick choices on grounds of popularity or liturgical expediency. One must ask hard questions of the music and of ourselves: 'Is this hymn/song realistic about God?' 'Is it realistic about the world?' 'Can we expect our congregation to sing it with conviction?' The answers to these questions might lead us to throw out some cherished favourites, but ultimately we will be doing our congregations a service.

Secondly, our choice must take into account liturgical considerations, foremost amongst which is the framework of the Church's year. The Archbishops' Commission, on a fact-finding tour, discovered a church which on Easter Day had one Easter hymn, one Passiontide hymn, one for Ascensiontide, and one for Pentecost[1]—can such liturgical ineptitude be excused?

Most hymnbooks are helpfully arranged (at least in part) according to the liturgical year, as are many choir anthem books. Lectionary themes offer a useful guide in the choice of music, and most hymn books include lists of suggested hymns for the ASB Lectionary.[2] If a service forms part of a preaching series, subject and scripture indices will come into their own.[3] Whatever the type of service, musical items should contribute to the overall theme.

Where music occurs within a service is largely a matter of liturgical common sense. An offertory hymn at Parish Communion, for instance, should be long enough to do its liturgical job. A 15-minute gradual anthem is inappropriate, as is a 20-minute group of songs between the sermon and the creed. Modern service books give sensible suggestions for the use of music, but one must always beware lest the placing of music become predictable. Is it necessary, for instance, always to have music to cover liturgical movement? It is good to sit back and rethink the place of music from a liturgical standpoint, and to borrow ideas from elsewhere. Coventry Cathedral's practice of following the sermon with a short organ voluntary is one that many churches could usefully adopt.

Thirdly, the choice of music should be governed by musical criteria. If there are not the resources to do a piece properly, then it is better to do

---

[1] *ITWH*, p.47.
[2] See D. Barker, *The Hymns and Songs List* (Hodder & Stoughton, Sevenoaks, 1992), and R. Leaver, *Hymns with the New Lectionary* (Grove, Bramcote, 1980). For users of *Mission Praise*, see Peter Bannister's index of Sunday themes and topics (published as part of *Church Leadership Pack no. 20* (CPAS, Warwick, 1993)).
[3] e.g. the Scripture index in *Hymns and Psalms* (Methodist Publishing House, London, 1983).

something else than to attempt the impossible. Complex music performed badly does not honour God and usually depresses those who attempt to perform it. Equally, banal and simplistic music should be avoided for the same reason. One should ask how well items are known by the choir/music group and congregation, and whether they can be learned easily. A congregational practice before the service is often a workable option, and can be a positive step towards bridging the gap between choir and congregation. It is also worth addressing the question of style. Some churches give each service its own musical character, while others prefer to include a mixture of styles within the same service. The likes and dislikes of the congregation need to be taken into account, as does the extent to which these need challenging.

Hymns and Songs

I have already written about the relative merits of hymns and songs. Choosing them is an important task and deserves careful advance planning. Last-minute choice usually yields a severely limited diet of hymns and songs. Advance planning enables a broad range of material to be sung and guards against over-use of individual items. A realistic scheme is to plan in 3- or 4-month blocks, on the basis that one would plan the thematic content of services on a similar timescale. Advance planning allows others time to make suggestions, and ensures the choir has ample time to prepare. Hymn lists should be kept, preferably on disc, for ease of cross-referencing from one year to the next and for future planning. New items should be introduced fairly regularly—though at the right time (i.e. not when the church is full of visitors).

Psalms and Canticles

The Psalms are a distinctive ingredient of Anglican worship. They form a direct link with the worship of our Jewish ancestors and run the gamut of human experience and faith. Yet in many parishes, they are never sung. This is largely because in many people's minds they have become synonymous with Anglican chant, and there are now few churches which have the resources to sing Anglican chant well. The alternatives to chanting are accessible to most churches, whether they have choirs/music groups or not. Many psalms are available in metrical form[1]: though metrical psalms can appear to be no different in idiom from hymns or songs. A distinctive style is responsorial psalmody, in which the congregation sings a refrain between verses from the choir/music group or a soloist. Responsorial psalms are easy to learn, and can be performed convincingly with minimal musical resources.[2]

Until recently, canticles had a limited definition within Anglican worship. With the ASB and the subsequent offerings of the Liturgical Commission, the range of canticles has broadened considerably. Most are portions of Scripture, while others have been newly composed. Despite the demise of Mattins and Evensong, there is considerable scope for using canticles in the Eucharist—often as a welcome change from a hymn or psalm. Good canticle settings, though, are hard to find, especially for the newer texts.

[1] See *Psalms for Today, Songs from the Psalms* (Hodder & Stoughton, London, 1990).
[2] See *Psalms for the Eucharist* (Mayhew-Macrimmon, Great Wakering, 1984).

Other Music

The breadth of musical style in many churches today is something that would have been unthinkable 15 years ago. Perhaps the single most significant arrival has been Taizé music, which has considerable appeal, across denominational boundaries and amongst those on the Church's fringe. Its musical flexibilty is a great strength, as are its liturgical possibilities. It can function equally well as a communion meditation, as a background to sung or spoken intercessions, or as a response to Scripture.

Much of Taizé music's appeal lies in the use it makes of instruments. The potential of instrumental music in worship is something which has scarcely begun to be tapped. Many churches still use nothing other than the organ, and those which have a music group seldom employ it other than to lead singing. There is a need for English churches to adopt a 'Lutheran' view of music in preference to the 'Calvinistic' outlook most of us have: where music is relegated to the status of servant to a text.

Music for Choir and Music Group

The development of music groups in recent years has brought a welcome rediscovery of shared musical ministry. There is the danger, though, that a music group can assume the 'separateness' of a professional choir. Churches which aim for a mixed diet of church music are perhaps best served by both choir and music group, though hard work is needed if the groups are to coexist happily and work together.

In addition to enabling the singing of the whole congregation, most choirs and music groups will perform on their own as a means of facilitating reflective worship. It is vital to be clear when and how this should happen. Communion might not be the best time for a choir anthem or group song, for instance. Worshippers might reflect more constructively on such a piece as a gradual. If the congregation is hesitant about psalm-singing but the choir is competent, a psalm or canticle can be sung reflectively. A short choir item or song to underline the theme of a reading or sermon, too, can be highly effective.

Many people who sing or play in church do so because they are musicians. Such people need musical challenges—something which is seldom recognised. While one should not attempt music beyond a group's capabilities, singers and instrumentalists should be encouraged to give of their best at the highest possible level, and directors of music should include sufficiently taxing music in the repertoire (whether traditional or modern) to do justice to their members' capabilities.

Who Chooses?

An Anglican minister has what Canon B20(2) calls 'the final responsibility and decision' in choosing music for worship. He/she is also required to 'pay due heed' to the advice of the organist or director of music. In other words, the responsibility is shared. The Canon guards against both, clergy who 'think they know best' and organists who are determined to hold a church to ransom. How shared responsibility works out in practice will vary according to the parish, and the experience and gifts of the vicar and the organist.

One approach is for the organist to draw up a draft music list for a specified period and for this list to be discussed with the incumbent (and any other interested party). A final music list is then issued, from which neither organist nor incumbent is to depart. A variation would be for the incumbent to make the initial choice.

Planning by committee irons out personal preferences which can threaten to dominate a music list, but involves the investment of a considerable amount of time from a number of people. It is perhaps more efficient to involve a committee at the initial planning stage (i.e. ideas for the three months ahead) or at the draft stage before the final list is produced. Any form of collaborative planning is time-consuming, but its rewards are considerable in terms of the balanced diet of music and worship it yields.

SHORT BIBLIOGRAPHY
(of works mentioned in the text)

Archbishops' Commission on Church Music, *In Tune With Heaven*, *[ITWH]*, (CHP/Hodder & Stoughton, London, 1992).
Karl Barth, *Wolfgang Amadeus Mozart* (Eerdmans, Grand Rapids, 1986).
Jeremy Begbie, *Music in God's Purposes* (Handsel Press, Edinburgh, 1989), 'The Spirituality of Renewal Music' in *Anvil*, 8/3, 1991, 227-239 .
Colin Buchanan, *Encountering Charismatic Worship* (Booklet on Ministry and Worship no. 77, Grove Books, Bramcote, 1977).
Deryck Cooke, *The Language of Music* (OUP, London, 1959).
Doctrine Commission of the Church of England, *We Believe in the Holy Spirit*, *[WBHS]* (CHP, London, 1991).
William Edgar, *Taking Note of Music* (SPCK/Third Way, London, 1986).
Edward Foley, *Foundations of Christian Music* (Alcuin/GROW Joint Liturgical Study no. 2, Grove Books, Bramcote, 1992).
Richard Griffiths, 'Religion and the Arts' in *Theology*, 95, 1992, 5-9.
Daniel Hardy and David Ford, *Jubilate!* (DLT, London 1984).
P. H. Lang, *Music in Western Civilisation* (Dent, London, 1942).
John Leach, *Liturgy and Liberty* (MARC, Tunbridge Wells, 1989).
Robin Leaver, *Music as Preaching, [MP]* (Latimer House, Oxford 1982), *The Work of John Marbeck* (Courtenay, Appleford, 1978).
Robin Leaver and James Litton, (ed.), *Duty and Delight* (Canterbury Press, Norwich, 1985).
F. R. McManus, *Liturgical Participation: an ongoing assessment* (Pastoral Press, Washington DC, 1988).
Leslie Olive, 'A Worship Song Analysed' in *Music in Worship*, 37, 1986, 6.
Stanley Sadie, (ed.), *The New Grove Dictionary of Music and Musicians, [NG]* (Macmillan, London, 1980).
Robin Sheldon, (ed.), *In Spirit and in Truth* (Hodder & Stoughton, Sevenoaks, 1989).
G. van der Leeuw, *Sacred and Profane Beauty* (London, 1963).
Geoffrey Wainwright, *Doxology* (Epworth, London, 1980).